PoEmotions
BLACK HISTORY
THE DEEPER THE ROOTS

Poems of Sadness, Defiance and Reflection That Shaped Black History

Patrick L.C. Meade

Copyright © 2021 Patrick L.C. Meade

All rights reserved. No part of this book may be reproduced, stored, or transmitted by any means—whether auditory, graphic, mechanical, or electronic—without written permission of both publisher and author, except in the case of brief excerpts used in critical articles and reviews. Unauthorized reproduction of any part of this work is illegal and is punishable by law.

Print ISBN: 978-1-950685-86-8
Ebook ISBN: 978-1-950685-87-5

Thank you for your support
Enjoy and be blessed

TABLE OF CONTENTS

Dedication ix
Introduction xi

Part 1 – Centuries of Grief and Struggles 1

When They Came 2
Bodies in the Ocean 3
Red & Black 4
If They Were Tried 6
The Scarred, Mangled Banner 9
Mother Emanuel 14
Man of Visions 16
Soldier of Truth 17
Educated, Liberated 18
The Devil's Punchbowl 19
Illusions of Freedom 21
Bloodsport 23

Part 2 – The 1900s to Now 25

Coontown 26
2,151 Days 28
Man in the Whirlwind 30
Black Wall Street 32

Bad Nigger 34
Decatur Street Plantation 36
Rock n Roll 37
Payola 39
Before Rosa 41
Love is Love 43
Not Your Nigger 45
Good Trouble 47
A Time for Martyrs 49
715 51
Latasha 53
Madiba 54
What Happened? 56
King Chad 58
The Black Man's Prayer 60
The Black Woman's Prayer 65

Part 3 – Black Lives Matter 69

More of the Same 71
Things Ain't Getting Better 78
Mr. Officer… 79
The Knee 81
The Final Straw 84
Momma (Is this a Dream?) 87
Yet and Still… 89
Why We Scream 91
Letter to Gianna Floyd 93
Hi Karen… 94
Exhalation 96

Part 4 – Responding to Ignorance 99

Don't Talk Bad about my Mama 100
What Year is This? 102
Slavery was NOT a Choice 104
Seriously? 106
What Took You So Long? 108

Part 5 – Soul Food (The Synopsis) 109

What We Gave You 110
Mother Africa Deserves an Apology 111
Black King 113
Black Queen 114
Blessed Earthly Vessels 115
Our Race 117
Juneteenth 118
How We Got Over (And Will Keep Getting Over) 120
Thank You God 122

About the Author 123

DEDICATION

To those that fought, served and marched to
pave the way for this generation
May this honor you

To the youth of today who are and will carry
on that legacy with dedication
May this inspire, inform and enlighten you

For everyone that reads these words, may you forever be blessed

INTRODUCTION

This is a follow-up to *PoEmotions Black History: Our Origins, Our Struggles, Our Future* (2018). Some of the poems here will sound very similar in message and tone to some of the selections from its predecessor, which was the intent when I put this book together. It keeps its common theme of poetic expression of the African American experience as I have seen and learned from years of reading books such as *On the Real Side: A History of African American Comedy* by Mel Watkins, school lessons, and through various media outlets.

The sections have been separated by centuries that I believe have relevance in the shaping of Black History, positive and negative. *Centuries of Grief and Struggles* are my interpretations of what I learned about the lives of Black people from approximately the colonialization of Africa until the end of the 19th century. *The 1900s to Now* addresses issues and people in this most recent century while also paying respect to those that had a positive impact on Black culture, which is also done in the preceding section. A lot of the selections in *The 1900s to Now* are written in a narrative that a Black person may have felt internally during those times. *Black Lives Matter* has some poems that speak on the Black Lives Matter movement and some of the cases that helped inspire it. *Responding to Ignorance* is my attempt at tackling some common misconceptions and otherwise ignorant statements that were made publicly in previous years. *Soul Food* contains my own thoughts or anecdotes that I chose to offer on certain things.

Nothing that I say in this book should be taken as offensive. My goal is simply to express my feelings through poetry and get you, the reader, to think about these subjects. It is great to always go back and review certain events in history. By doing this, we can learn what was done wrong and what could have been corrected.

Overall, I hope that you truly enjoy this book. May something in it inform, inspire, and enlighten you in some way.

~Patrick

PART 1
CENTURIES OF GRIEF AND STRUGGLES

WHEN THEY CAME

Life was full of joy
A feeling that could not be explained
Happiness could not be contained

But when they came…

These strange vessels came across the sea
These strange vessels came across for me
These strange vessels would encase me

And those chains…

Cold to the skin
I am in the hold of sin
These men looked so nice
But are cold from within

Packed us into confined spaces
Like animals in tight cages
For reasons that were quite baseless

My home is now growing father away
As these strange vessels drift farther away
From my motherland and her hands
What will await me in this other land?

BODIES IN THE OCEAN

Some jumped in to take their own lives
Some were tossed in after they died
Victims of the cramped spaces & diseases
Cast away like they had no meaning

Left for the sharks who swam their way
Some bodies sank to the ocean floor to decay
One can only wonder
What was the total number?

Swept up by the current
As the slave ships kept going
As the ocean waves kept flowing
For those still on those ships, pain kept growing

What awaited in the New World
They had no way of knowing

RED & BLACK

Many of us forget that the Native Americans were the first casualties of European colonialism. The land that they had founded and welcomed the Europeans too with open arms would be taken from them. In some ways, the Native American was the original Negro.

The Native Americans had the land, culture and resources, just like ancient Africa. After the colonialists came, they claimed everything as their own. Over time, their true origins would be largely forgotten for years that followed. Again, this is not meant to sound offensive. This is just what happened.

However, many Native Americans and African slaves violently fought back…

The red man & the black man became intertwined
When their history began to be redefined
By colonialism that put them in a prism
For most of them, it felt like a prison

This was how the Europeans plan went down
Take the land from the Indians & have the African till and plow
Early America was founded on their blood & sweat
The powers that be made profits with no regret

But the red & black man did not like that
So, they decided to strike back
If they were to die, they would die fighting back

Seeing this, the overseers tried to divide & conquer
Have the reds & blacks fight each other
Let them bring about their own slaughter
Then, they would step back and watch it
While still putting more cash in their wallet

Red & Black may be different
But in history, they are the same
They got caught in the fray of the colonialism game

America got founded as they paid the price
Their history from that day on would be a long fight

IF THEY WERE TRIED

A hypothetical about The Founding Fathers of America

Before I go into this poem, I believe that an explanation is in order so that no one takes the message that I am trying to convey in the wrong light.

This poem, like all the others in this book, is not meant to be or sound anti-American in any way. I love my country and am proud to be an American. America is the greatest country in the world due, in part, to what our Founding Fathers like George Washington, Thomas Jefferson and Benjamin Franklin contributed. However, there was a dark side. While America (then known as the 13 Colonies) won their independence from Britain, there was still slavery for Black Americans. Most of the Founding Fathers that I mentioned were slaveowners before, during and after the American Revolution. Some of you who may be reading this may not have known that before. Please feel free to do your own independent research on this subject.

As I mentioned before, this is strictly a hypothetical poem about the relationship between The Founding Fathers and slavery. Please, do not take this in the wrong light. The purpose of this is to simply stimulate deep thinking and possibly spark a conversation about the history of America.

Thank you and enjoy…

The Founding Fathers indeed fought for independence
Unfortunately, there were some exceptions
Though freedom for them became common
Blacks were still in bondage

In a sense, the Founding Fathers committed perjury
Claiming that they were freeing all men
But acting like they never heard of me

Before that, they placed blacks in forced labor
Day by day, dumping on their overworked backs more favors

Add to that, the endless cases of assault
Every time we had the lash crash on our back
The slaveowners said it was our fault & that we should have obeyed
If we asked for freedom, they ignored what we had to say

But what if they were brought up on charges?
What if they were prosecuted for being heartless?

The charges - False imprisonment, forced labor and rape
Assault & murdering those who tried to escape
They may have been charged for perjury
For preaching freedom while they were hurting me

Exploitation was the norm
In any weather, cold or warm
Making so many feel scorned

If the Founding Fathers were tried, some
would have never become President
Maybe America would have gotten to truly set the precedent
Of all men being created equal
Sparing us from racism and its endless sequels

If they were tried, the course of history would have been changed
Maybe race relations today would not still be so strange

THE SCARRED, MANGLED BANNER

Much like the previous poem, I believe what I am about to say here deserves an explanation. Once again, this is to ensure that the message I am conveying does not get distorted for senseless purposes.

Most people are aware that Francis Scott Key wrote the national anthem for America, *"The Star-Spangled Banner."* However, most people may not know that Francis Scott Key was a slave owner. At one point, he was quoted to have said that "blacks are a distinct and inferior race of people, which all experience proves to be the greatest evil that afflicts a community."

To provide a better context of where I am going with this, Key wrote the lyrics to The Star-Spangled Banner after observing The Battle of Fort McHenry on September 14, 1814, which was part of The War of 1812 between America and Britain. It had been launched by then President James Madison in order to gain control of Britain's Canadian colony. In the midst of this, several colonial slaves and some freed black Americans had actually volunteered to fight on the side of Britain and volunteered to aid one of their admirals, George Cockburn. The reason why is because they had not been given the guaranteed freedoms that the Declaration of Independence had stated.

Cockburn would train most of them to be soldiers and they carried out various raids that destroyed a number of slave plantations. One famous incident was when these black volunteers, who would become known as The Colonial Marines, torched The White House. Some may view the actions of the Colonial Marines and other blacks who chose to leave America as treason. However, is it really treason if they were never properly given their God given rights that were promised to them in The Declaration of Independence, which by 1814, had been in place for thirty-eight years? Were they really being treasonous if after some of them fought for America during The Revolutionary War and were yet still seen and treated as being inferior by those officials who wanted independence from Great Britain? Apparently, Francis Scott Key felt that way.

There is evidence of this in the forgotten third verse of *"The Star-Spangled Banner."* Few people know that there are three additional verses in our national anthem besides the popular first verse that is always sung. The second half of Verse 3 reads…

"No refuge could save the hireling and slave
From the terror of flight or the gloom of the grave
And the star-spangled banner in triumph doth wave
O'er the land of the free and the home of the brave"

It seemed as though Francis Scott Key was rejoicing in the fact that many blacks, who were Americans, though not given any rights, had been killed during this war. When I learned this information, I was taken aback. So, I decided to write the following selection…

"No refuge could save the hireling and slave
From the terror of flight or the gloom of the grave
And the star-spangled banner in triumph doth wave
O'er the land of the free and the home of the brave"

Those were the words of Francis Scott Key
Confirming that when the Founding Fathers
said "All men are created equal"
They forgot me
He said that we couldn't be saved
We deserved to rot in the grave

Francis Scott Key's delusions of race went further
Behind the scenes, he was a racist pervert
Calling them an inferior race of human beings
Calling them the greatest evil that afflicts a community

No wonder Kaepernick kneeled

When our national anthem in 1814 was written
America was fighting The War of 1812 with Britain
A small detail of the conflict that's been hidden
Is that freedom for the black slaves was given…by Britain

Yes, it does sound ironic
Because it was European colonialism that got slavery started
But even they saw the duality of colonial America's heroes
How could they preach freedom & forget the Negroes?

Colonial slaves volunteered to fight for Britain
Because in the new America, freedom for them was still forbidden
For them, it was not the land of the free
So, could you blame them for choosing to leave?

For just wanting real freedom, they were seen as traitors
When those that advocated for independence were really haters
So, Mr. Key considered them lower than dirt
To him, they deserved death & to be laid in Earth

No wonder Kaepernick kneeled

Then, when Mr. Key was Washington's D.A.
He allowed blacks & abolitionists to be slain
Feeling they deserved death since they wouldn't behave
Does this sound like they were protecting the home of the brave?

Francis Scott Key saw them as an item for profit
Any semblance of equality for blacks, he'd block it
Because he owned his own slaves & plantation
He felt blacks should suffer social castration

But America, my country 'tis of thee
Sweet land of liberty
Of thee, I will still sing

You are still my home
I will still claim you
If anyone asks me where I want to live
I will still name you

If Crispus Attucks believed it was worth giving his life
I believe it's worth claiming as mine

However, for everyone's sake
Just have the courage to admit your mistakes
Though Francis Scott Key is painted as a patriot
He was clearly full of hatred

He never showed an ounce of respect
To those who America still owes a great debt
So, before we paint certain people as heroes & idols
Restudy history to make sure they're worthy of those titles

MOTHER EMANUEL

A tribute to one on the oldest churches in America

Mother Emanuel was born amidst slavery
It was a place to run for those to worship bravely
Surrounded by hatred based on race
But not once did she lose faith

Its children were ripped from this house to face the lash
While the white man smiled & laughed
Those same men ran in to steal its possessions
Trying to prevent black progression

Because the greatest fear of those men
Were people they didn't understand
So, they judged them by their skin
Not what's within

Then when a former slave was brave to rebuild this house
Those who were racist wanted him out
Denmark Vasey was his name
Wanted to free those who were once in chains

White supremacists feared insurrection
America going in the wrong direction
Blinding themselves with lies
They sent spies in Mother Emanuel to see who should die

Vasey was taken and hung
Into Mother Emanuel, Hell would come

This house of God was burned down
Temporarily silencing church sounds

It would be rebuilt by faith
But destroyed again by an earthquake
But it would rebuilt again & stand for the next century
People of all races began entering

Praise you Mother Emanuel
For going through all Hell
To stand and give praise
To God's holy name

MAN OF VISIONS

Nat Turner was born in the year of a slavery uprising
By three, he was saying things that were surprising
He spoke of visions he had seen
His mother hadn't given them to him in a dream

People called him a prophet
Even from a young age
Nat Turner believed that when he grew
He would free the slaves

By the time he was a man
Turner's words would spread broad
Bringing dozens of his brothers
To his great cause

Telling them that in order to get flight for freedom
Together they had to fight for freedom
They fought and fought as hard as they can
Until they were rounded up by the white man

Nat Turner would hang after being tried
It was a sad day when this preacher died
Though this was the end of Nat Turner's life
More & more would pick up his fight

SOLDIER OF TRUTH

Her real name was Isabella Baumfree
She understood everyone should be born free
When she became a full-grown woman, standing 6 feet
She had a booming voice whenever she would speak

She took the name Sojourner
Willing to go further
Like a soldier in the field
Guarded by God's shield

She took the last name of Truth
Which she tried to commute
To everyone from the elderly to the youth

She would walk tall
Testifying defiant
Oppression needed to be taken from those tyrants

She also argued for gender equality
Knowing that women have so much quality
Isabella was a soldier of truth walking proud
She was a soldier of truth talking loud

Though we have different races, genders and names
She believed we should all be treated the same

EDUCATED, LIBERATED

Frederick Douglass was born a slave
Refused to be held down by chains

A slave owner's wife taught him to read & write
Through that act of kindness, he saw the light

When he found freedom, he would go & speak
His speeches would have a far reach

By his intelligence, he spread his message through print
An example of what education & dedication can get

Mr. Douglass fought for liberation
Throughout this nation
Moving & speaking with determination

Before Garvey
Before Malcolm
Before Dr. King
Frederick Douglass showed the world what
an intelligent black man can bring

THE DEVIL'S PUNCHBOWL

Natchez, Mississippi became a destination
For slaves who finally achieved emancipation
Those in charge saw the population get out of control
So, a wicked scheme would unfold

Camps were built for men to labor
Where their newly gained freedom couldn't be savored
Conditions were worse than on the plantation
What did they do to deserve this damnation?!?

Families were separated again
Women & children would suffer in pain
Dying of starvation & disease
While men slaved until they collapsed on their knees

The biggest part of this confusion
These camps weren't owned by the Confederates, but by the Union

Wait a minute...
I thought the Union was fighting for me
Hold up...
Was the Union lying to me?

Why did they separate us?
Why did they continue the hate of us?
Even after many died, the hate didn't stop
The Union army had the corpses buried where they dropped

What was the point of the Civil War?!?
Blacks were still scorned
Many that were there begged to return to the plantation
They thought even that was better that this abomination!!

Rotting corpses fertilized peach trees
Literally growing Strange Fruit that is bittersweet
Pray that those poor souls finally found peace
Away from a world that refused to let racism cease

ILLUSIONS OF FREEDOM

1863: Blacks were declared to be free
But equality was something some whites still couldn't see
Mixing of the races was something they hated
So, they plotted and schemed to keep blacks segregated

Some resorted to dragging Blacks across state lines
To states where they could maintain slave times
Power of profit overcoming humanity
Everyone chose to ignore this insanity

Nearly a century earlier
Some Blacks fought for America's freedom
But for some racist whites
They still wanted us to see none

Separate jobs, separate schools
Were some of their new rules
If we gained intelligence like them
To them, that wouldn't be cool

So, hate & division kept on
We were continuously stepped on
Some could never make a living
Respect & dignity weren't given

Jim Crow practices would flow to the next century
Convinced that free blacks were a disease festering
So, they tried to kill it at the source
When blacks reached for opportunities, they met closed doors

They weren't even allowed to vote in elections
They were still viewed as the lowest form of natural selection
Blacks may have started to feel that life was a curse
Little did they know, things would get worse

BLOODSPORT

An exhibition that became a sick tradition
Racists beating black men into submission
Blood, disfigurement & death were its features
The KKK were real violent creatures

Killing for sport
Blood spilling in quarts
What was all of this carnage for?

A black man asking for honest work?
A black man not calling a white man "Sir"?
Saying a curse or trying to vote?
That's why they killed blacks in droves?

Meanwhile, so called good Christians turned deaf, dumb and blind
Their silence gave white mobs permission to keep practicing genocide
To continue murderous acts as a game
How could those men have no shame?

Making blacks afraid to walk
Making blacks afraid to talk
Yet, they claimed this was all for God
What an evil facade

PART 2
THE 1900S TO NOW

COONTOWN

*About a section in Greenwich Village
at the start of the 20th century*

Blacks came to New York to start new lives
However, they discovered that hate resides
In the North as it was in the South
Landlords would overcharge them to live in a house

Though blacks came in droves
Few of them would get to stay in homes
Greenwich Village would get new fame
When it was given a new name

Coontown

Charles Dickens said dogs would not go to lie there
Some blacks would only die there
Beaten by mobs on false pretenses
High society looked away, senseless

People tried to cover up these New York crimes
By writing lies in The New York Times
Saying our songs & dances were accepted in the best class
While not giving us jobs to get cash

Keeping darker skin folks in poverty
Feeling that giving us wealth would be bothering
The status quo Jim Crow said whites ought to keep
The philosophy Willie Lynch said had to be

Coontown was not where blacks meant to live
White neighbors never meant to give
Anything to them, including fortune
To them, we were an unwanted burden

2,151 DAYS

*About the 1st Black World Heavyweight Boxing Champion
Jack Johnson & the search for a Great White Hope*

For 2,151 days
For 51,624 hours
Mainstream media in America would scour
To find one man to stop a mighty Black tower

Someone whose skin was fair like theirs
A representative of the ideals they shared
They wanted a Great White Hope
To make the dreams of the Black man disappear like smoke

Then, the hero of the Black man was Jack Johnson
Knocking everyone out in the ring they walked in
Punching racism in the face
Wearing the heavyweight title around his waist

But back then, the media could not take it
Feeling that the dream of the Negro had to be taken
They wanted to find someone, anyone
To knock Black hope to Kingdom Come

They thought a victory for Jack Johnson
Was a victory for the Black man as a whole
They said, "Hell No!"
This villainy has to go

Especially when Jack threw it back in their face
Dressing chic & dating women with a white face
Figuratively, Johnson said "Fuck you!"
The way you have treated blacks sucks too

So, despite his lavishness
If you look at the bigger scope
Amidst racist savageness
Jack Johnson was a symbol of hope

For 2,151 days, the Black man felt anything was conceivable
Anything was achievable
Anything, like racism, is defeatable

MAN IN THE WHIRLWIND

Rising from poverty to inspire
Marcus Garvey would speak words of fire
Encouraging a new generation
To rise up with the right education

Educating blacks about their homeland
So that they could take their own stand
Saying "Africa is your mother"
Encouraging them to take pride in their skin color

Imploring us to wrap ourselves in the red, black & green
Allowing ourselves to be seen
Red for the blood we bear
Black for the skin we wear
Green for the land we share

However, along the way he got confused
Meeting with the Klan who caused the abuse
Other black leaders would scream "This is hypocrisy!"
Feeling Garvey's words were feeding into their philosophy

They further said "Garvey's no leader or friend
He's only helping the Klan's end"
As fast as the world spins
He stayed in the whirlwind

But his positive words still ring true
For us to take pride in what we do
So that we don't live in misery
Let's embrace our own history

BLACK WALL STREET

Blacks travels to Oklahoma on wagons, horses & trains
To begin life anew with much needed change
Tired of the oppression of Jim Crow's slavery
Getting up & moving out took bravery

Nearly 10,000 lived there
Nearly 10,000 would give there
They had dreams they wanted to bloom
So, they built businesses that would boom

There were stores & markets to get food
Pool halls, beauty parlors & barber shops were there too
At the same time Harlem started its Renaissance
Greenwood in Tulsa, Oklahoma had everything you would want

They built their own houses
Built their own restaurants
Built their own theaters
They had so much to flaunt

Greenwood was visited by W.E.B. DuBois
Deep down, his heart had to be filled with joy
The Souls of Black Folk were prospering
Centuries of oppression Blacks seemed to be conquering

However, some of their white counterparts
Didn't share the same feelings in their hearts
Instead, they got a different spark
They felt Black Wall Street had to be torn apart

After rumors of a young Black man harassing a white girl went around
White mobs felt Greenwood should be burned down
The Black community feared for the young man's life
So, they rushed over to stand & fight

The white mob grabbed their guns
A fresh battle had begun
Shootouts carried over to the rising Sun
Mostly Black blood would run

But then, the white mob would conspire
To set Black Wall Street on fire
Everything the Black community ccreated
Ended up being incinerated

They even dropped bombs from the sky
So many innocents would die
One could only wonder why
Was it all out of a false sense of pride?

Accusing a black teen of harassing a white girl with no proof
Using it as an excuse to go loot
Destroying businesses & lives
Ruining a community that once shined bright

Black Wall Street is now a memory
Of potential that was meant to be

BAD NIGGER

*About racist views of African Americans who
dared to defy perceptions of them from racists*

These were the 4 criteria to describe a Bad
Nigger during the vaudeville era
- Disregard for life & death
- Pride in sexual virility
- Extravagance in dress & possessions
- An insatiable love of having a good time

They made them up for comedy routines
Because of some blacks who through history they seemed
To challenge racist norms
So, they threw these up to quell storms

The likes of Nat Turner caused long before
Saying we really had nothing to live for
Claiming that all we care for in life
Is a party & sleeping with another wife

As for the steps
We took between life & death
They said that we could not care
If tomorrow we breathe our last breath

They would later try to use Jack Johnson as an example
To boost their egos to a size that is ample
But Jack dared not to care
Whenever he got hateful stares

In the years that followed, others would take the lead
Martin, Malcolm, Baldwin & Ali made others take heed
That past stereotypes were all lies
Making them open their eyes

However, racist minds were resistant
Throwing up walls at their own persistence
Blinded by their own ignorance
Calling our role models bad niggers with no significance

But the more walls they were making
Were the more walls we were breaking
More pride in ourselves
We slowly, but surely, were taking

Saying we could dress like you
We could sex like you
We could flex like you
So, you can keep being spiteful

God is on our side
We do not have to hide
We will keep showing our pride

DECATUR STREET PLANTATION

About a theater in Atlanta during the early 20th century

Black singers sought freedom when performing in a theater
Only to discover racism inside there was hotter than a heater
One place in particular on 81 Decatur Street
Was the worst place for a black performer to plant their feet

The owner named Charles P. Bailey
Ran the theater like a plantation daily
Harassing women with help from the cops
If one woman told him to stop, she would get popped

Bailey beat up Bessie Smith
Before having her thrown in jail
It would make a black person wail
Decatur Street was a block away from Hell

When Ethel Waters stood up to him, she was called a bitch
So, Ethel decided that the plantation had to be ditched
But old Charles Bailey could not give her an inch
All he cared about was getting rich

No respect
No honor
No shame
Making profit from his cold games

ROCK N ROLL

The evolution of the gospel sound
The evolution of the blues we sang
Whenever we were down
Into a music that would be felt from miles around

Though blacks & whites were still kept apart
White teenagers would still step out after dark
Dancing to the music that was like no other
Made by some talented brothers

Though Elvis got pushed as the rock n roll king
Chuck Berry was the true father of this rock n roll thing
John Lennon even said this music would be named after him
Every artist that followed framed their game after him

Before The Beatles & The Stones flowed over
Chuck Berry was telling Beethoven to Roll Over
Before Hendrix let his guitar rip
Chuck duckwalked while playing guitar riffs

If Chuck Berry was the father, Little Richard was close to God
The originator, the emancipator, the quasar
Many would imitate his screams and hollers
Listening to how they did it, they should've bothered

Before rappers, Richard was a true G
Singin' 'bout the Tutti Fruttis with good booties
Like *Good Golly Miss Molly*, *Lucille* & *Long Tall Sally*
White kids were dancing from the suburbs to the valley

There were others like Bo Diddley & Fats Domino
If you didn't know their names before
Now, you ought to know

Listen to their old school songs
You won't do wrong
To research the founding blocks that founded rock

Hail King Chuck & King Richard
Made money, but should've been richer
Hail King Bo & King Fats
If you take away the obvious, you would've seen that

They were the OG Macks
The original kings of rock
Black brothers that made white girls scream a lot

So, at the altar of rock's original reverends
Bow down & give them reverence

PAYOLA

About how the music industry tried to lessen the impact of African American musicians & make more money for themselves

Rock n roll was filled with soul
But music industry bosses would try to take control
Whenever someone like Little Richard would rock a mic
The bosses listened and wanted to paint it white

Asking for Elvis or Jerry Lee Lewis
Tutti Frutti will be a bigger hit if one of them do it
They had Pat Boone cover the song
Someone should have told them that it was wrong

Taking from the masters & not giving them credit
Just to sell their own gold records
These were the games that were played
How could no one feel any shame?

But there were a brave few like Alan Freed
Who believed blacks in rock was something we need
So, he played Little Richard & Chuck Berry
Their influence on the kids, to their parents, was scary

What was the industry ever to do?
Paint black records white is what they would choose
While Elvis made the youth tap their shoes
His sound was still rooted in rhythm & blues

So, they could have painted black records in white
The sounds from Mother Africa would still seep into sight
Though parents would get uptight
It was sounds of blackness that kept the kids up at night

BEFORE ROSA

Before Rosa Parks refused to give up her seat on the bus
There were 2 other sisters who started a fuss
Though these incidents happened nearly a decade apart
These 2 women had a lot of heart

First, in July of 1944
Morgan Kirkaldy could take no more
Fed up with the conditions she was living in
Others like her treated as second class citizens

So, when she refused to give up her bus seat
She symbolically said that racism must cease
Saying I deserve to sit where I choose
My natural freedom should not be abused

Nearly 11 years later in 1955
A month before Emmitt Till was killed for a lie
99 months before Rosa Parks refused to give up her seat
Another brave girl symbolically said that racism must cease

Claudette Colvin was only 15 years old
In her young life, she saw America was so cold
So, on March 2, when she was leaving high school
She silently yelled that racism wasn't cool

Cops decided to arrest her
Cops tried to suppress her
But they didn't succeed
Claudette walked free

Although Ms. Parks' bravery is remembered in history
Women like Morgan & Claudette shouldn't be a mystery
It's important to do some research
What you learn can have some worth

LOVE IS LOVE

About interracial marriages

Does it matter if I am black and she is white?
Is that a reason to threaten my life?
Am I really destroying what makes her pure?
I'm just telling her, "I want to be yours"

Love is love

If she loves me despite my race
You need to get out of my face
Let us have our space
So we can share an embrace

Love is love

I do not love her because she is white
I love her because she is human
We need to see each other in that light
Or our humanity is ruined

Love is love

I love her smile & her heart
Do not tear us apart
God brought us together
He is the only one that our bonds can sever

Allow us to love despite our appearances

Allow us to love despite our differences
You are in no position to judge
So, do not hold a grudge

Love is love

NOT YOUR NIGGER

Inspired by the words of James Baldwin

I am not your nigger

That was what Brother James said
You are probably wondering what Mr. Baldwin meant

He meant that we are not beasts or vermin
God created us to complete a purpose
Of living, teaching & breathing freely
Being proud of what we achieve

Brother James spoke facts
When he said America got rich off the backs of blacks
Our sweat, our blood & our tears
Helped shape America for countless years

That was the message Baldwin brought outward
Whether in America or the halls of Oxford
Raindrops of truth came from his mouth in downpours
Whose nigger am I? Not yours!

I am my own man & take my own stand
Though I am separated from my homeland
I am no animal always on the roam
So, let this truth be known

No hurtful words will define me
No hurtful words will confine me
I am not a reflection of Hell
Instead of insulting me, you should be checking yourselves

GOOD TROUBLE

In memory of Representative John Lewis

If someone asks what "good trouble" means
It doesn't mean coming up with an illegal scheme
Good trouble means standing up for what is right
Good trouble means fighting for justice with all your might

That's something that The Boy from Troy did
That's the way The Boy from Troy lived
He was only five foot six inches, but he became a giant
When racism surrounded him, he refused to remain silent

John Lewis was inspired after listening to a young King
Believing in his heart that he could do the same thing
After Emmitt Till died over a lie
John felt the need to rise for a fight

A fight that would be a difficult task
But God would give him the strength to last
God gave him the strength to endure
God knew that John's mission was pure

He sat in
He preached strong
He marched on
He did it all for so long

He endured beatings and faced death
Any moment, he could have breathed his last breath
His blood covered many streets
But he kept fighting so we would not face defeat

He bravely crossed the Edmund Pettis Bridge
Each step meant more hope he would give
To a generation in need of inspiration
Showing them what happens with dedication

He epitomized Black Lives Matter before it was a catchphrase
He shined in the light and never lacked grace
Lewis took his passion to the halls of Congress
Over time, he became its conscience

Without John Lewis taking his stand
Barack Obama may have never said "Yes we can"
Without John Lewis, I may have never written these words
So, to Mr. Lewis, praise is eternally yours

Thank you for marching
Thank you for preaching
Thank you for fighting
Thank you for teaching

That good trouble can change the world
Just like you did

A TIME FOR MARTYRS

*Dedicated to some of the people who were
killed during the Civil Rights Movement*

For Medgar Evers, who fought as hard as Malcom & Martin
Shot in front of his house before he could walk in
He fought for his people to not live in pain
Fighting to bring about a true change

For 4 young girls, killed going to church
For being taught to love anyone who is hurt
No matter their creed or color
They learned Jesus' plea to love one for another

For 3 young men who tried to get people of any color to vote
Giving black youth a symbol of hope
Their fate was sealed by the Klan's hate
But they could not erase their legacy that stands great

For Malcolm, who saw his fate coming
But he chose to move forward, instead of running
Though he was killed by his own who were misguided
His teachings still fill our bones & we cannot deny it

For Martin, who got to see The Promised Land
Before having his life stolen by another man's hand
You taught us all to hold fast to a dream
That blacks & whites can live in harmony

For them and other brave sisters & brothers
Let the world discover
That you did not die in vain
Thank you for showing us that we won't live or die in shame

715

In honor of Hank Aaron

715 is only a number
715 is only a statistic
But the thought of a Black man reaching it
Made some go ballistic

Some didn't want to see Hank Aaron break a legend's record
In their minds, it meant Armageddon
America's pastime would head into a recession
The image of white pride was threatened

So, they hurled threats at Hammerin' Hank
They called him names
They wanted him to hide in shame
All because of a record

This was after Jack Johnson knocked out racism for 2,151 days
This was after Jesse Owens stood victorious in Hitler's face
This was after Jackie Robinson first broke
barriers on the baseball diamond
This was after Muhammad Ali first dazzled in the ring, shinin'

Despite the hate, Hank kept dropping the Hammer
All the haters could do was stammer
Proving their words never mattered
It was inevitable that a record would shatter

Then came the date – April 8
America would see something great
The bat cracked the ball
It flew over the wall

715!!!

As Hank rounded the bases
2 college kids ran beside him with smiling faces
If only all of America shared the same mind
Showing us that we should be colorblind

But in that stadium, they didn't see races
All they saw was greatness
Black excellence once again trumped hatred
This was truly a moment that was sacred

The hits kept coming
Specifically, 40 more
755 was the final tally on the board
Hammerin' Hank would forever be adored

Although his record would be surpassed
His legacy can't be matched
Unlike his successor
Hank's record still stands pure

So, to Hammerin' Hank Aaron
The home run king
You forever stand through the ages
Your legacy we sing

LATASHA

Dedicated to Latasha Harlins, a 15-year-old girl who was shot and killed in a convenience store in South Los Angeles

A young girl died for no reason
Shot from behind with no meaning
Young Latasha wanted some juice
She did not look to rob, steal or shoot

Latasha put the juice in her backpack & was ready to pay
Sadly, the store clerk saw it in a different way
She only saw her as a thief
A shot in the morning sent a family to grief

The little lady in the liquor store panicked
Taking young Latasha's life for granted
All for a bottle of juice
That was no excuse to shoot

Young Latasha would have had more living to do
She had much more giving to do
But now, she is hanging with Tupac in *Thugz Mansion*
Though we should not forget about what happened

Tragedies can happen all over misunderstandings
Which should teach us to come to understandings
Improving communications will prevent other lives from termination

MADIBA

A tribute to Nelson Mandela

To you Madiba, we give praise
In situations where others would've run, you stayed
Though South Africa was afflicted by apartheid
You refused to run to the far side

You fought and fought
For power cannot be bought
People couldn't be separated because of race or class
So, you went to the frontline and held fast

Though you were incarcerated for 27 years
You could not be silence
You were prepared to die
If fate had desired it

After 27 years, you emerged victorious
The day you returned was glorious
You overcame not with force, but with brains
Because of this, you sought change

For this cause, God had selected you
In prison, Mother Africa protected you
With her prayers that she sent above
She & God showered you with unconditional love

Now Madiba, you are at rest
Thank you for giving your best
For the betterment of your people
In dark times, you rose & became a hero

As Mr. Obama said, you now belong to the ages
As one of the greatest figures in history's pages

WHAT HAPPENED?

About the state of hip hop

Skilled rappers through history, I have seen some
But today, some rappers just speak dumb
Just saying stuff to get records sold
Ignoring rap's essence & stories that were told

What happened?

Nowadays, most rappers just mumble
Syllables just tumble
Verses sound incoherent when you hear it
But record companies give them clearance

What happened?

What happened to the alliteration and clear articulation?
That the greats would say with dedication
Now in the modern age, anything that most rappers say
Instantly gets air play

What happened?

Some songs sound the same
Shout out their city, the crew they claim
The women they screw & the size of their chain
Nonsensical songs instantly get you fame
Despite the small scope of their brains
More dollars get attached to their name

What happened?

The dead MCs must be turning in their graves
If they heard the things some rappers say
When comparing the new school to the greats
Their skills cannot relate

Some OGs were natural poets
Some had the best flow
They all had lyricism
If you hear it, it shows

Some had all 3, plus the best punch lines
Nowadays, most rappers sound like they bust rhymes at lunchtime

Talking with their mouths full
Words don't even sound full
Will they ever match up to the greats?
Very doubtful

That is just my opinion
I'm entitled to it
That's just the way I feel
I'm sticking to it

KING CHAD

In honor of Chadwick Boseman

From playing Jackie with #42 on your back
To *Get On Up* embodying the Godfather of Soul
To playing Thurgood Marshall, fighting for equal rights for Blacks
You were a powerful sight to behold

But when you became King T'Challa, everything changed
In millions swelled a great sense of pride
You forever changed the game
Our joy was impossible to hide

When we saw you, we saw us
We saw what we could be
If in ourselves & God we trust
We can also be kings and queens

You did all these things while battling a disease
Without any complaint
You still carried yourself with ease
You still carried yourself with strength

You were a warrior in every sense of the word
You have now become a legend
You now rest comfortably with the Lord
You have now gone home to Heaven

Let us not forget what your roles symbolized
Purpose, strength and grace
Let's not forget what helps our dreams materialize
Purpose, strength and faith

Thank you, King Chadwick
God and Bast hold your hand
Thank you, King Chadwick
May your memory forever stand

Wakanda Forever!!!

THE BLACK MAN'S PRAYER

Inspired by an email my mother sent me many years ago

Introduction (Anonymous voices)

Voice 1: Hey look at him. Can you believe someone could look like that? His parents must be as ugly as him.

Voice 2: Yo nigga, what's up? You got your clothes out a dumpster or something?

Voice 3: You ain't worth shit? Man! Look at you, stupid ass nigga.

Voice 4: What the hell are you looking at man? Yeah, that's what I thought, nigga. Don't start nothing, there won't be nothing.

Voice 5: Nigga please. You better walk on before something bad happens to you man.

Black man: Lord, I try to lay down to rest
But deep in my heart I'm still so depressed
So now I got to get these feelings off my chest
In the hopes that you can relieve some of my stress

God, I have a question
About a misconception
So now, please give me some direction
Dear God, why did you make me black?
Why did you make me something that the world wants to hold back?

God: Why did I make you black?
Now what in your mind would make you ask me that?

Black man: Because people think I'm useless
I feel so used
Why do people think that?
I'm so confused
When people see my skin, they say I should be abused
So, God tell me, is all this the truth?
God: People talk about you because they only see the external
They don't recognize the person that is internal
Their hearts being filled with original sin
That's why they're so quick to judge you by the color of skin

Black man: Yeah, but black's the color of an eye when someone's hurt
It's the color of darkness, the color of dirt
Black's the color of grimy hands & grimy feet
The color of darkness & a tried beaten street

God: But your color is the same as soil that grows the food you need
To feed your offspring in your caring
Plus think about the stallion & panther
Such majestic creatures because of their dark features

They are beautiful like you
But I hold you closer & love you more, this is true
So please ease your mind & relax
Cut yourself some slack
You're beautiful because I made you black

God: Now are you satisfied?
Have your fears been pacified?
Do you understand why I made you black?

Black man: Yeah, I'm starting to understand
But there are some more things that you have to tell me man…

You know my own people mistreat me, why?
Sometimes I feel like I want to cry

Whenever I see someone walking in the street
I go to holler at 'em, they won't look at me
And then people talk about my skin type
Some say I'm too dark or I'm too light

I hear this mess every single day & night
Lord you have to know all this stuff is not right
Then they make fun of my hair & what I wear
Why did you create someone that always gets a hateful stare?

God: I made you the color of coal from which diamonds are formed
The color of oil that keeps everyone warm
Why do you think every nation would kill for it?
It's so valuable, just like you

As for your hair, I made it so fair
In the texture of lamb's wool, so must care
Because I am the shepherd who watches over the sheep
And I'll also watch over you when life's distresses get deep

Black man: Maybe so, but there's another
thing that I'm trying to figure out

That nasty word that comes out of every black man's mouth
Sometimes it makes me want to scream & shout
So God tell me, what is this word all about?

Every time I hear this word, the way it's said gets bigger
Hearing it in rap songs & major motion pictures
People always want to pull it off like a trigger
When they say my first name's "Stupid" & my last name's "Nigger"

My friends use it every time that they call on me
Eventually it's used more than "I," "you" and "the"
Today they try to make sound so cool
Its meaning is something that isn't taught enough in schools

"Nigger" was used to call blacks animals & cannibals
Saying that we were worse than Hannibal
How could they be so blind to put that out of their minds?
I keep asking myself time after time?

So now I'm going to fall back in this chit chat
Why do people call me nigger God?
Answer me that

God: They call you out of your name because they were raised in hate
A sin that sometimes isn't that easy to shake
So remember, whenever anyone calls you a…
N.I.G.G.E.R.
You are much more, so never ignore
The heritage that you came from
Those that paved the way for you
Those that made a way for you

I gave you the mind of Malcolm X and his intellect
So that when you grow, it's done in excellence
Buried in you is the passion of a Martin Luther King
Who had a dream that you & others were destined for greater things
Pushing for more than just bling bling & fancy things
Because in my love, you have all that you need

I gave you the articulation of Barack Obama
The same quality that I installed in your mama
That's why people marvel at you whenever you teach or preach
Because when you speak, you're able to reach each

So, hold your head high & kiss the sky
Telling anyone who hates on you to walk on by
You've got more living to do
The greatest creation that I put in this world is you!

So, the next time you look in the mirror
I want you to see that I made you in the image of me
That's why I made you black

THE BLACK WOMAN'S PRAYER

You thought I forgot about the black women? Oh no, I can't forget about you. So, this is for you.

Black woman: Dear Lord, I come to you
With a question that I hope you have the answer to
Because it's been bothering me & troubling me
Frustration bubbling inside of me

God, why did you make me black?
Something that the world always wants to hold back
Nobody cuts me slack
They just see my skin & a brick wall in front of me they stack

God: This question, why do you ask?
The faith in your race, why do you lack?
You've always been on the right track
So why do you ask, "Why did I make you black?"

Black woman: Because people look at me in a crazy way
Black is what people are labeled when other want to stay away
Black's the color of a shadow cast
The color that falls when a day has past

God: Dear sister, why do you cry?
Your skin is the color of the midnight sky
If you look deep inside, you'll realize
I put the glitter of stars inside your eyes

Black women: Well then, why do people make fun of my hair?
The clothes that I wear
Everyone gives me a hateful stare
Why are my bone structure & my lips so thick?
And why does everyone stare whenever I move my hips?
Why do people think I'm useless?
Can you tell me what my true worth is?

God: The texture of lamb's wool is what I used to make your hair
So in my eyes, it'll always be fair
Now for the clothes you wear
People don't stop to think
That what you wear makes you unique
Your style is a part of your mystique

So, stop stressing over this, be at peace
I made your bone structure thick to withstand the tests of time
Don't make yourself blind
You're fine just like a glass of wine
Look yourself in the mirror & know that you're mine

Now this about your lips that are tender
They're thick so that when you're kissed, the man will remember

Black woman: Maybe so, but I still think you need to make a change?
Can't you just redo creation, make everyone the same?

God: Now if I did that, it would defeat my purpose
And what I'm telling you would be a waste of verses
The rainbow's colors are in every nation
But when they're mixed together, you're my best creation

That's why you're black
God: Is that all you want to know? Are you ready to go?
Black woman: Not yet because I've got
something else to ask before I forget.

There's still one thought that always makes me twitch
Something that's worse than a seven-year itch
God, can you explain to me real quick
Why on Earth some people want to call me bitch?

God: Because some people are ignorant
Don't stress over this or throw a fit
Just keep carrying yourself with grace
Don't put yourself to waste
Keep a smile on your lovely face

Just don't forget those who paved the way for you
Made a way for you
So, you could break through

In you is the courage of Rosa Parks
Your mind is sharp & you'll make it out of the dark
You're articulate like Maya Angelou
Your words always flow every time you go

You have class & grace like Michelle Obama
If people ask how, say "I got it from my mama"
But don't be a prima donna

Just remember to keep your head up high
Carry yourself with pride
And never ever hide

The true beauty that you have inside
Something that you're carry until you die

Knock down the wall that was stacked
Because you got it like that
That's why I made you black

PART 3
BLACK LIVES MATTER

Much like my introduction into *If They Were Tried* and as I did for the introduction to sections with this title in *PoEmotions Black History – Our Origins, Our Struggles, Our Future*, I believe that an explanation of what you are about to read is necessary here. This is to ensure that the messages that I am trying to convey do not get distorted or misunderstood by anyone.

The poems in this section reflect the emotions that I was feeling at the time of instances where an African American was killed during an altercation with police. High profile cases such as the Rodney King beating in 1991 and deaths such as those of Amadou Diallo (not far from my home), Eric Garner, Michael Brown, Tamir Rice, Freddie Gray, Walter Scott, Kalief Browder, Alton Sterling, Philando Castile, Sandra Bland, Ahmaud Arbery, Breonna Taylor & George Floyd made me very sad and angry.

When I wrote the poems you will be reading here, I reflected on these instances. Though the death of Kalief Browder was a suicide, an argument can be made that what endured being locked up in Rikers Island and the trauma that he had to endure during his incarceration and afterward contributed to him taking his own life. What made me feel even worse about each case was the fact that those responsible for those deaths were not punished sufficiently. They may have been reprimanded, suspended or fired. However, they were not sentenced to serve any kind of jail time.

These were primary inspirations for the "Black Lives Matter" movement that has occurred in recent years. To cope with my own feelings of sadness, anger and at times hopelessness and fear of my own mortality, I wrote the poems mentioned before as well as 4 others.

There of course have been other instances of African Americans dying after altercations with police officers for relatively minor instances. However, in the heat of the moment, the officers perceived these men as a bigger threat than they really were. The end results were that families lost their loved ones.

MORE OF THE SAME

1991:
4 cops beat down Rodney King in L.A.
Caught on tape, but they got to skate away
Verdict: not guilty
Though their hands were filthy

I wasn't even 2

February 4, 1999: The Bronx
Not far from my house
4 cops sprayed 40 shots, 17 snuffed Amadou Diallo's life out
They mistook him for someone who committed a crime
When they encountered him, they thought he was reaching for a nine

They thought he would cock it
But when he dropped it, it was just a wallet
But apparently, the jury didn't feel they were to blame
What a damn shame

I was 9 years old

November 25, 2006: Queens
3 cops shot 50 shots at Sean Bell
Instead of a wedding, he's being prepped for a funeral
Cops walk free
Any of this new to you?

I was barely a senior in high school

February 26, 2012: Sanford, Florida
By now I'm 22
Trayvon could've been my little brother too
Shot dead by a dude looking for trouble
Zimmerman wasn't even a cop
But they still let the case drop

More of the same
What a shame

7/17/2014: Staten Island
Eric Garner is choked out on the sidewalk
Camera phones on for the city to watch
13 times, this father of 6 pleaded for breath
Until it was depleted and left

No CPR before a trip to the ER
The cop who did it never sees being behind bars
Things only got worse 3 weeks later
As casualties of police brutality grew greater

August 9, 2014: Ferguson, Missouri
Another young brother who could've been mine by blood
Had his life snuffed out by a gun
Even if there was a little scuffle or tussle
Mike Brown didn't have to die for such little trouble
I was about to turn 25

11/20/2014: Brooklyn, New York
Akai Gurley gets shot in a dark stairway
The culprit was a rookie cop
In prison, he could have been locked
But no, he was allowed to walk

3 days later: Cleveland
Tamir Rice, another who could have been my little brother
Was only 12 when his life was smothered
Horse playing with a gun cops were told looked fake
But that little detail didn't matter to the Jakes

Could've ran Tamir down driving at high speed
2 slugs to the chest & the little brother bleeds 'til he's deceased
More of the same
It's a dirty shame
So many snatched away in this dirty game

4/4/2015: Charleston, South Carolina
On the anniversary of MLK's death
5 bullets caused Walter Scott to breathe his last breath
Just because he chose to run
He didn't have to die by a cop's gun

8 days later: Baltimore
Freddie Gray was the victim of a rough ride
He never committed a rough crime
Another senseless death in these tough times
6 cops caught a case
But all of them walked away

6/6/2015: The Bronx
Kalief Browder may have taken his own life
But in his short life, he endured trauma and strife
Arrested for taking a bookbag, though there was no proof
Was thrown in solitary confinement & robbed of his youth

His mind slowly decayed
As by the justice system, he was betrayed
By the time he was finally released, the damage was done
The trauma in his brain was too much to overcome

Can we really put fault on Kalief?
Should he really be blamed?
The justice system is truly to blame
How could they have no shame?

7/13/2015: Waller County Jail, Hempstead, Texas
Sandra Bland may have taken her own life
But three days earlier, she was afflicted with strife
She was harassed over a traffic stop
When she was locked up, the guards didn't keep standard watch

If they did, Sandra may still be alive
Her family wouldn't have so much agony inside
She became another sad statistic in an increasingly cruel game
More of the same, such a shame

7/5/2016: Baton Rouge, Louisiana
Alton Sterling was selling CDs gets taken down to the ground
Soon his chest explodes from 6 gun sounds
Thought there was a gun in his pocket
But there was none to raise or cock it

The next day: Falcon Heights, Minnesota
Philando Castile was merely driving with his girlfriend
When he got caught in this vicious whirlwind
He gets stopped by a cop, then gets shot
Recorded on Facebook Live & the world watched

On top of that, another witness was his girlfriend's daughter
If a bullet went the wrong way, she could
have been caught in the slaughter
He had a permit to carry a weapon
But he wasn't even reaching for it
This was cold blooded murder, but the courts ignored it

How much more wrong can go on?
As a girl tells her mom to stay strong

August 30, 2019: Aurora, Colorado
Elijah McClain was just walking home
Blaring music, minding no one's business but his own
But, because he was introverted & wearing a mask
Police felt he should be harassed

Elijah was brought to the ground with little to no reason
Soon, he started having trouble breathing
Police choked him out & drugged him to stop his "agitation"
Permanent damage was done with no reparation

February 23, 2020: Brunswick, Georgia
Ahmaud Arbery goes for a run
Only to come across 2 men with a gun
He was struck down because he was thought to be a criminal
Their prejudgment bringing on more ridicule

Have we learned nothing from the sins of the past?
Do we have to keep putting you on blast?
If we can, we will, if we must
Because more & more, we are losing more trust

March 13, 2020: Louisville, Kentucky
Breonna Taylor was just sleeping in her house
When the cops came & broke her door down
Claiming the house was full of drugs
Then suddenly, filling it with slugs

Breonna ended up another casualty
Killed by cops so callously
No drugs were found
But another innocent is getting put in the ground

Too many sisters and brothers have died
Too many fathers and mothers have cried
Too many cases like these have been ignored & tossed aside

We don't say Black Lives Matter just out of rage
It's to say we finally want a change
Whenever we see these and other scenes
We get painful flashbacks like PTSD

We remember when the Klan caused the black man pain
Only to be allowed to do it again
We remember when police sprayed water on little ones
Even then, no justice would come

So, when we see more of the same in this age
That's why we explode with rage
We've suffered through this before
We don't want to suffer through this anymore

There's no other way to make it plain
No other brother or sister's life should be taken in vain

THINGS AIN'T GETTING BETTER

Things ain't getting better
They're just getting worse
Every other week, another black hearse
Carries another black casket to be laid in Earth

As they prepare another burial plot
Life doesn't change for some cops

When another black corpse is laid to rest
Cops just keep getting their checks
As the corpses' hands are crossed on their chest
Cops get a new badge on their vest

My stomach turns
My heart burns
When in God's name will the wheels of justice turn?

MR. OFFICER...

Written after a personal experience with a police officer

Mr. Officer
Take a good look at me
I mean, take a real good look at me

Do I look like a threat?
Do I look like I will harm you or anyone else?

Look beyond the fact that I am blacker than night
That my voice booms off the wall
That my hair is a certain way

Do not place me in one of your stereotypes

I respect your authority
But you should respect my humanity

You only see the color of my skin
You should see the content of my character

So, Mr. Officer, let me enlighten you
I am not a criminal, thug or thief

I am a man
I am a teacher
I am a poet

I am a friend to somebody
I am a brother to somebody
I am a lover to somebody

Though I am not perfect
I am a child of God

THE KNEE

Nowadays, taking a knee is such an issue
That if you do it, someone will diss you
Claiming that you do not love this country
Calling you an ungrateful S.O.B.

People forget, or choose to ignore, why it started
Interpreting it as being cold hearted

One person did it to protest police brutality
More importantly, protesting America's duality
In regards to race, taking a knee is deeper
It was never about the flag or selling sneakers

It goes back to the slavery days
With all the evils of slavery's ways

Blacks took a knee in the fields from exhaustion
Forced to work until they were heaving & coughing
From hours working in the heat
Tilling soil in the rain, snow, hail & sleet

Calices & blisters formed on our hands
Muscles got weak & we could not stand
To catch a breath, we took a knee
Slaveowners said, "Boy! Get on your feet!!"

Fast forward over a hundred years
After crying more than a hundred tears
Racists used similar tactics
Brothers & sisters still took action

Whether it was sitting in restaurants until they were served
Some racists got unnerved
Screaming & wailing, "Get on your feet!!"
Before assaulting us & throwing us on the streets

Elsewhere, others took a knee to pray
That racism would finally go away
But they were branded out of order
Had dogs loosed on them & hosed with water

With clubs, they were bludgeoned
Given bruises & concussions
Because to them back then, we were nothing

These & what I said before was why blacks took a knee
But we were still seen as S.O.Bs

The irony of all of this seems
Racists always wanted blacks on their knees
Telling the black man to kneel to suppress them intellectually
Telling the black woman to kneel to impress them sexually

They wanted us to kneel against our will
But when we do it to protest when one of ours is killed
We are in the wrong
We are disrespectful
NO!

We are trying to have our message get through

Before you call us S.O.Bs
Take time to research history

Do you think Crispus Attucks was an S.O.B.?
If he was not the First to Die in Boston, America probably would not be
Do you think Rosa Parks was a harlot for sitting in the front of the bus?
When all she was doing was speaking for us

Was Malcolm X an S.O.B. for all his preaching?
When he was just exposing racism's false teachings
Was Martin Luther King an S.O.B. for the times he marched?
When he was just trying to lead his people from the dark

Protesting racism by taking a knee
Is as patriotic as saying, "Don't tread on me!"

Let me get this through…

I don't hate this country or the troops
But I have to speak the truth
It may hurt like pulling a tooth
But I have to tell it to you

If that makes me an S.O.B., I will be one proudly too
I will be like the others who fought for truth
If I am an S.O.B. for taking a knee to speak loud
Then I will stand up and say…

I am an S.O.B. for God and I am proud!!

THE FINAL STRAW

Memorial Day, two thousand twenty
This was the final straw for many
Not just for Blacks, but people of all races
Demonstrating & screaming that racism is baseless

George Floyd had a knee pinned behind his neck
4 times, he pleaded to regain his breath
For 8 minutes, 46 seconds, his pleas were ignored
When the world saw this murder, we couldn't take anymore

The world heard us scream "Enough is Enough" too many times
After we have seen too many crimes

They heard us say "No more!" after
Trayvon Martin
Eric Garner
Michael Brown
Tamir Rice
Walter Scott
Freddie Gray
Sandra Bland
Alton Sterling
Philando Castile
Elijah McClain

Now, after George, Ahmaud & Breonna were slayed
The world screamed with us that justice cannot be delayed
Blacks should be allowed to breathe
Blacks should just be allowed to be

Enough is enough!
We are screaming for real change
Enough is enough!!
We are tired of feeling surreal pain

How many more have to die?
How many more have to cry?
How much longer must we hear lies?
Saying that things will be different this time

Blacks have had knees on our necks when we were locked in chains
Back when we were forced to be slaves
We had knees in our necks when cowards in white sheets
Lynched us & burned our houses in the night heat

We had knees on our necks in the 1950s
We had knees on our necks in the 1960s
Damn it, enough is enough!
Those knees need to start lifting

Get the Hell off my neck!
Give me my damn breath!
I have earned a right to live
I deserve some damn respect!!

What was done to George Floyd was the final straw
We can no longer put our movement on pause
Enough is enough & things need changing
Enough is enough & things need rearranging

Blacks may have started as slaves in this country
But we have fought wars for this country
We have brought culture to this culture
We always give our all to this country

Now, it is time for America to give to us
Give us justice
Give us equality
Above all, give us real love

MOMMA (IS THIS A DREAM?)

A poem from the perspective of a child

Momma, what's going on outside?
Why is everyone trying to fight?
Is everything alright?

Momma, what went wrong?
Did something go wrong?
Do you know what's going on?

Why are cars on fire?
Why is smoke rising higher?
Is it a dream?

Why are all the people mad?
Why are all the people sad?
Is it a dream?

Momma, why are the people yelling?
Momma, are you able to tell me?

Momma, why are they throwing things?
Why are they breaking things & taking things?
Why are they so mad?

What are the police shooting at them?
Why are the police shooting at them?
Is it a dream?

What is going on?
Did something go wrong?

Momma, before I go back to sleep tonight
Will everything be alright?

YET AND STILL...

Yet and still, some are still seen as threats
Blacks should not fear taking every single step
We should not fear that today we will take our last breath

We may be Black, but we are still human
Why is there so much confusion?
How I wish this was just a cruel illusion

A man gets shot 7 times in front of his kids
Can we imagine the trauma that will follow them as they live?
It may be hard for them to still forgive

Cops assumed Jacob Blake was going for a weapon
Giving them an excuse to use aggression
Now he ends up paralyzed and everyone is stressing

For me, it causes post-traumatic stress disorder
Because years earlier, Jacob Blake could have been me
Shot for no reason, left laying in the street

Each time they say things will change
The next episode is the same
Replayed on the news again & again

But, to those like me who see these scenes
Though they will cause you to cry & scream
Don't let them discourage you or your dreams

If you have to march to get your point across, march
If you need to preach to teach & reach, preach & teach
In all things, we must never cease

Though so many years have passed, we still have much to prove
Though ignorance abounds, we must not be moved
God is still on our side & we will not lose

WHY WE SCREAM

*Inspired by the song Why We Sing by
Kirk Franklin & The Family*

Someone asked a question
Why do we scream?
When we say "Black Lives Matter"
What do we really mean?

Someone may be wondering
When we scream as one
So many times, we've cried
Wondering when a change will come

We scream because we're angry
Seeing too much misery
We're tired of injustice
That's the reason why we scream

We've seen too much injustice
We've seen too much wrong
Although we still forgive
It's happened for far too long

So, if somebody asks you
Is this all just for show?
Stand up and be a witness
To tell the whole world "No!"

When we learn to love each other
So racism is no more
We will sit altogether
In harmony forevermore

LETTER TO GIANNA FLOYD

Dear Gianna, only 6 years old
You have seen that the world can sometimes be cold
But I saw a video with you & your daddy the other day
I was drawn by something you had to say

As your daddy held you up
His precious little girl
From high on his shoulders
You said, "Daddy changed the world!"

Now, the change is being seen
Not just in America, but overseas

Britain, France & Italy
Mexico, Germany & Denmark
Your father touched their hearts
Igniting in them a spark

That change can finally come
That peace & justice can freely run
Peace on the left & justice on the right
People making it happen with all their might

So, young Gianna, as you grow
May you come to know
That the world isn't what it seems on screens
No matter your color, you can achieve your dreams

So, in his own way little girl
Your daddy indeed changed the world

HI KAREN...

Hi Karen, I think we should talk
I've noticed you watching me as I walk
Do you assume I will do something wrong?
Do you assume I will do you harm?

Before you make more assumptions that aren't true
Let me please explain a few things to you
I may be black, but I am not a crook
There's no reason for me to get a harsh look

I work very hard for my money honey
The way you're acting is making you look like a dummy
I have a family & my own life
Why do you want to cause such strife?

I'm merely minding my business
You attacking me is a sign of a sickness
Not the physical kind, but one in your mind
If you can't recognize it, you must be blind

Karen, I am not your enemy
If you gave it a chance, we could be friends indeed
I have no intent to assault or molest you
For you to assume that is disrespectful

Even though you call yourself super sweet
The way you harass me makes you look super mean
You claim to be high class, but your attitude comes from a sewer
If you cannot respect my humanity, you should leave in an Uber

Take a long ride home
Your thoughts you need to collect
On the way, learn a little about respect
Instead of the bad reputation you are about to collect

Think before you act
Look before you leap
Now, as you walk the streets
The thought is that you are a creep

All because you chose to profile me
Despite your efforts, you will not defile me
So Karen, respect me and my truth
Maybe in return, I can respect you

EXHALATION

Breathe in, breathe out
There were many times when we let out a shout
Shouts of anger and frustration
Over systemic racism in this nation

2020 was the final straw
From the chaos came louder calls
For true justice to come despite a badge
So many times, it felt something some couldn't have

Then on April 20, 2021, the world waited for a verdict
Everyone knows where they were when they heard it
An officer was found guilty of murder
Becoming headline news on Internet servers

Across the nation, many were able to exhale
There was a much different ending to the usual tale
For so many years, many families were left in pain
Feeling that the deaths of their loved ones were in vain

To them, justice was denied
But on April 20th, justice and closure was supplied
Though the verdict won't bring George Floyd back
A huge cloud was removed from their backs

A claim rang true for George's little girl
Her daddy did change the world
There is hope that other cases will end the same way
Hopefully families will feel less of the same pain

Of course, more cases like this will happen
More already have
The ones that have come are still tragic
More families are left sad

However, for a moment on April 20th, the nation exhaled
A different ending came to the same tragic tale
The jury agreed that George Floyd's life mattered
It never deserved to be shattered

That moment should not have been a time for exaltation
It should have been used for exhalation
That moment should have continued reparations
For the wounds that are still present in this nation

PART 4
RESPONDING TO IGNORANCE

In 2018, there were several high-profile people that made ignorant and flat-out stupid statements in regards to African Americans. Whether it was a comedian with a successfully relaunched TV show making a comment of Twitter about the physical appearance of an official in President Barack Obama's administration, a prolific rapper making a claim on TMZ Live that slavery was a choice or even the 45th President of the United States referring to African countries as "shithole countries." Then, a famous news anchor who transitioned to getting her own morning talk show made a claim that when she was growing up, it was okay to wear blackface if someone was dressing up as an African American. All the while, I just shook my head and wondered what the Hell was wrong with these people.

I decided to put my frustrations to the paper in my poetry notebook and convert them to what you are reading right now. This is my response to the ignorant and stupid statements that I previously mentioned. Hopefully, you will be enlightened and informed to the truth.

DON'T TALK BAD ABOUT MY MAMA

Another ballad to Mother Africa

A while back, a certain man
Allegedly took a certain stand
Apparently, he had to make it known
That certain countries are shitholes

Bringing on controversy and drama
By slandering the children of Africa & their mama
So, I want to make it plain
Don't go dissing Mother Africa's name

Despite the bad images rarely seen on TV screens
That's not what Mother Africa was or is meant to be

She nurtured fantastic beasts
Her children once accomplished fantastic fetes
She birthed kingdoms & cultures so rich
But now, someone essentially called her a bitch

The reason she's looked down on is because of how she was left
Raped, naked & a victim of theft
Her children turned to slaves to till the land
If they disobeyed, slaveowners would whip or kill the man

Those countries (her children) that were called troubled
Are still that way long after they were turned to rubble
Blacks are still murdering one another
Disregarding each other as sisters and brothers

Whether it's killing for diamonds and riches
Or slaughtering elderly women they assume are witches
Terrorists taking girls from homes & schools
Forced to be sexualized under evil rules

Because of the few that's been seen or heard
Certain people feel some way & have the nerve
To speak & preach bad about my mother
Because her children are poor, afflicted with AIDS & hunger

Though she's not in a common state
I still keep a common faith
That Mother Africa will once again rise
Mother Africa will once again shine

Just like in those days of old
Beaming with those rays of gold
Though her children are in a mess
They & Mother Africa will always be blessed

WHAT YEAR IS THIS?

Awhile back, someone had something to say
About someone because of the shade of her face

Tried to get a big laugh
But instead, caused a big gash
In a wound that hasn't been fully healed
In a wound that was never fully sealed

Could I just ask a question?
What year is this?
No seriously, what year is this?

It seems people still want to berate me
It seems people still want to degrade me
Thinking that it's funny to say I look like a monkey
Thinking I am dumber because of my color

So again, I ask, what year is this?

Because it feels like 1958
For pity's sake!!
What is wrong with people?
Racist jokes are worse than Transformers sequels

Every time we think this bad franchise will end
The same dumb plot keeps repeating again
Ignorant person who feels entitled
Makes a comment just to be spiteful

They were not funny in 1958 or before
They are definitely not funny now
It sounds worse than someone standing on the baseball grounds
Butchering the national anthem, grabbing their crotch & spitting down

People in 1958 did the same thing
Only with clubs, burning crosses & bullets spraying
People butchered The Star-Spangled Banner
By butchering black men in savage manners

Then, after they got their cheap kicks
They grabbed their crotches & spit
On a black corpse & lacked remorse
Then joked about it…of course

But this is what people need to understand…

Blacks got killed & their blood spilled over jokes like that
Blacks couldn't eat in a diner over jokes like that
Blacks couldn't use a public bathroom over jokes like that
Blacks couldn't get good jobs over jokes like that

So, to my brothers & sisters, keep your head up
Though people speak ignorantly about you, don't hate them
They're putting themselves in a mess
But you rise above because you were born blessed

SLAVERY WAS NOT A CHOICE

A brother said 400 years of slavery was a choice?!?
That we willingly chose not to lift up a voice?
How ignorant can someone be?
To suggest we no longer wanted to be free

What about those who dove off the ships?
Some of them mothers cradling their kids
What about those who rose to fight?
Burning plantations & escaping at night

If they really found solace in bondage
They would've kept working for the white man's profit
That's now how it happened in history
Pick up a book, school yourself and it won't be a mystery

You insulted those who paved the way for your dreams
Crispus Attucks, Nat Turner, Harriet Tubman, Marcus Garvey
Malcolm X & Martin Luther King
Jackie Robinson & Muhammad Ali

Would these legends & others been relevant?
If they said, "Freedom & equality? To Hell with it!!"
We want to be held under & worked asunder
Considered by racists as history's blunder

You fail to realize while your lips were flappin'
You've become a victim on the mental slavery
you say blacks are trapped in
You're a product of Willie Lynch's methods
Break the black man down 'til he destroys himself 'cause he's reckless

Though you've apologized since
I pray that you've realized this

Next time, check yourself before you wreck yourself
Humble your own hype before you become a stereotype
Of what & how some people see a black man
Straight up, that's just whack man!

Before you say something else stupid
To get the media buzzing
Stop, think about it
Then, just say nothing

SERIOUSLY?

Seriously?
It was cool to wear blackface?
You don't think it was ever in bad taste?

Seriously?
Are you being for real?
This is something really surreal

Here is a little education for your information
Hopefully this provides some clarification

From this, hopefully your thinking will be less outdated
Then, you will not say things so outrageous
Leaving me to ask where you're talking from – mouth or anus

Blackface was used in vaudeville
To further embarrass blacks who were killed
White actors painted their faces a darker color
Pranced around, bumbling & stumbling to
convey that darks are dumber

Bugged out eyes, wild hair, puffy lips
People saw that as entertainment
They must have been sick

Then, decades after it was considered dead
Somebody got it into their head
To say it was okay when she was younger
Not realizing that she was just sounding dumber

Blackface was used to dehumanize me
Blackface was used to further scrutinize me
Blackface was used as a way to crucify me
Blackface was used as a way to brutalize me

If you think it was cool
Then, I think you're a fool
You've been used like a tool
You should go back to school

I'm not biting my tongue
This truth I bring right from my lungs
Let it shine bright like the Sun
Let it bust out like a gun

Don't mock me with blackface
Because I don't lack grace
I'd be tempted to leave you with a smacked face

But I'm not going to embarrass myself
I'm not going to disparage myself

I'm going to never let up
Even though of this ignorance, I'm fed up
I love my real black face
So, I have to keep my head up

WHAT TOOK YOU SO LONG?

What took you so long to acknowledge the wrong
Of hundreds of innocent Blacks being gone?

Killed out of jealousy & false assumptions
Buried in mass graves as a sign of corruption
So many lives snuffed out for nothing
Over lies created for nothing

Why wasn't what happened in Tulsa taught in schools?
The sight of men treated worse than mules
Is enough to make any man seethe
Men not getting a chance to live or breathe

Why wasn't what happened in Tulsa taught in college?
Students needed to acquire this knowledge
That America had a dark side
Always giving a sharp eye to those with a dark hide

What took so long?
Was the reality of those crimes too harsh?
That they had to be hidden & locked in the dark?

Now, it's out in the air
People are now aware
So, spread the truth about the Tulsa Massacre
It's time to be fair

PART 5
SOUL FOOD (THE SYNOPSIS)

WHAT WE GAVE YOU

For centuries, some said we were insignificant
However, we gave the world things that were significant
It took Mr. DuBois' intellect to say it
Now a century later, I'm going to relay it

Black Americans gave you songs and stories
For the world to harmonize about their glories
Sometimes, the lyrics were soft as a light wind
It passed through this world with every slight spin

Black Americans gave America sweat and brawn
They have allowed the country to stand strong
Uncle Sam's hands couldn't have done it alone
So, we were worked to the bone

Whether voluntarily in battlefields
Or involuntarily in cotton fields
Black hands helped bring you freedom
Black hands helped you gain profit when you needed some

Finally, Black Americans brought the Holy Spirit
If you ever heard one of us pray, you'd hear it
Though you would try to claim God as your own
Claiming that to blacks, God was unknown

These and many more gifts we would give you
To help you, guide you & from the ground lift you
That's what Mother Africa taught us to do
That's what we chose to do for you

MOTHER AFRICA DESERVES AN APOLOGY

Initially, I was going to leave this out
But I couldn't and have to scream and shout

For kidnapping her seeds
For stealing their early dreams
For the endless nights she was forced to scream
Mother Africa deserves an apology

For scourging blacks with the crack of the lash
Forcing scars to crest in the aftermath
Then, you would just laugh
Mother Africa deserves an apology

For denying us freedom
When we really needed some
Setting up false laws to make progress pause
Mother Africa deserves an apology

For the harassments & beatings
Dealt out to her seedlings
The times you looked the other way as innocent blacks were slain
Mother Africa deserves an apology

Mother Africa can forgive, but she cannot forget
She should not live with shame & regret
An apology may not completely mend her heart

But it would be a decent start
Racism still exists
But it should not have to persist
So again, I insist

Mother Africa deserves an apology

BLACK KING

Don't let anybody shame you because of your race
You're an example of God's grace
When someone disses you over your color, pay them no mind
Brush that dirt off your shoulder & stay on your grind

You are a black king
Black strength
Black royalty
Friends may come & go, but you always act loyally

Some may joke & try to make you rage
But stay unbreakable like the skin of Luke Cage
Some may say your looks are frightening
But your fetes shock them all like Black Lightning

Racists may scream and holla
You have the heart of T'Challa
A Black Panther's heart beats inside, deep down
Though you're owed one, you don't need a crown

So, let those haters fall down the hill
Meanwhile, keep yourself real
Impress the rest with your intellect
Collect your checks 'cause you're the best & blessed

Then, everyone will wail and scream
All hail the king!!

BLACK QUEEN

Don't let anybody shame you because of your race
You're an example of God's grace
When someone disses you over your looks, pay them no mind
When they speak erratically, they make themselves go blind

You are a black queen
Black beauty
Black royalty
Friends may come & go, but you always act loyally

If people try to joke about your looks, it's because they're jealous
Your essence illuminates in others' presence
Whether you're dark chocolate, caramel or light brown
Tell those haters to pipe down

You don't have time for them
Don't waste your time with them
Let them fall down the hill
Keep yourself real

Be a Vixen that weakens hearts with looks that kill & sex appeal
Cast your own Storm that makes men wet with sweat
Let your beauty be that all giving light
Keeping your man cool on a misty night

Still impress the rest with your intellect
Collect your checks 'cause you're the best & blessed
Then, everyone will wail & scream
All hail the queen!!

BLESSED EARTHLY VESSELS

Inspired by II Corinthians - Chapter 4, Verses 7-10

Our earthly vessels are our treasures
Even if some see us as lesser
Although the days grow hard
Let our excellency be not of us, but of God

We may be troubled, but let us not be distressed
Let us not despair, though we are perplexed
Struggling to find the words
To explain why racism still occurs

We may be persecuted
But we will not be forgotten
We will keep rising up
We will not be downtrodden

People may try to cast us down
But we will never be cast out
Some may want to see us destroyed
We will just rise up & make more noise

Though we keep going through hardships
We must still let our light shine in darkness
We have to let it shine in our hearts
From us, God will never part

We have to hold to our faith
We have to lean on His grace
Suffering can only last for so long
We have to keep our feet planted so strong

We may bend, but hate must not break us
Ignorance must not shake us
The people must stand firm
We will not run or squirm

We will hold up our heads
We must stick out our chests
To the nations, we will address
We are not cursed, but blessed

OUR RACE

*Derived from For Every Race from
PoEmotions: God and Faith*

Our race is not a curse
God has blessed us with much worth
We must share the earth
We must uplift each other when we are hurt

Our race is beautiful
Our race is blessed
Our race is phenomenal
Our race must be our best

We are lovely in God's eyes
We should still walk by God's side
Let's teach ourselves not to judge
Let's try not to hold a grudge

God loves us all the same
So, let us do the same
Let's not wallow in shame
Let's lift up each other's names

Let's just be God's children
If we have faith in ourselves & God, we'll always win

JUNETEENTH

This is a date I only learned about recently
How important this day is in history?

But then again, it was likely was never taught
So, independently years later, it had to be sought
Fast forward to two thousand nineteen
My mind was experiencing an enlightening

Though in 1863, slaves were emancipated
Slaveowners felt Blacks should still be emasculated
Going so far as to drag them across state lines
Just for the sake of maintaining slave times

Slaves were brought all the way to Texas
To continue a practice that was racist & reckless
All for the sake of profit
All of this was nonsense

Then, 2 years later, on June nineteenth
True freedom came…finally!!
After Robert E. Lee surrendered
The chains of slavery were legitimately severed

Hence the reason Juneteenth is celebrated
It's the day Blacks in America were liberated
Even though Lincoln declared it to be in 1863
Narrow minded racists wouldn't let it be

Though America declared itself free nearly a century before
The freedom for Black folks was ignored

Now, we'll still celebrate July Fourth
After all, it was a date Crispus Attucks died for
If not for America, at least for his name
To ensure Crispus' sacrifice was not in vain

But if he could have seen Juneteenth, he'd be proud
Seeing that America may finally come around
Seeing Blacks as human beings
Letting equality be true indeed

Of course, between then & now, we've had many struggles
Between then & now, we've had many troubles
But Juneteenth is still a day to be proud
Juneteenth is still a day to shout out loud

We have seen so much
But we have overcome
We have suffered so much
But we have overcome

We have been scandalized so much
But we have overcome
We have been vandalized so much
But we have overcome

Many have tried to cast us in Hell
Through it all, we have prevailed
We are truly blessed by God
We will always rest by God

HOW WE GOT OVER (AND WILL KEEP GETTING OVER)

A poem of perseverance

With the blood of Mother Africa flowing through our veins
Reminding us of where we previous came
With the heart of Crispus Attucks
We refused to back up

With the grit of Harriet Tubman & Sojourner Truth
Guiding our feet to push us further to
Prosperity & freedom
When we really needed some

With the poetry of Langston Hughes
We got to say "We are America Too"
With the passion of Marcus Garvey
Feeding us pride when we were starving

With the right hook of Jack Johnson
With the mighty legs of Jesse Owens
With the left hook of Joe Louis
We were strong enough to keep moving

With the voice of Mahalia Jackson giving us faith
With the strides of Jackie Robinson running to home plate
With the courage of Rosa Parks not giving up her seat
Inspiring us to get on our feet

With Muhammad Ali's flash & flare
Swift on his feet, dancing on air

With the intellect of Baldwin, Malcolm & Martin
Whether it was writing books, speaking or marching

With the pride of The Black Panther Party
With Jesse Jackson saying, "I Am Somebody!"
With James Brown saying loud "I'm Black & I'm Proud!"
We weren't going to let anybody turn us around

With Obama saying, "Yes We Can!"
Reminding us well see The Promised Land
With screams of "Black Lives Matter!"
We refuse to let our lives shatter

Though we've carried loads as big as boulders
We've survived and gotten bolder
That's how we got over
That's how we will keep getting over

THANK YOU GOD

By Jaylen Jones Coleman

Thank you God for letting me be free
Thank you God for letting me be

For giving us hope in the hardest times
To let us sing songs about you in rhymes

Thank you God for letting me be free

We pray to you Lord to keep all peace
Just like you did in old time Greece

Thank you God for letting me be
For everyone to see

So once again I say…
Thank you God for letting me be free

ABOUT THE AUTHOR

Patrick Laurence Charles Meade is a teacher, musician, poet and author. He has a bachelor's degree in Childhood Education from The City College of New York. Patrick is also a musician at St. Paul's Progressive Methodist Church in the Bronx, New York, a position that he has proudly served in for over fifteen years.

Preceding this book are *PoEmotions: Poems of Life, Love, Faith and All Emotions* (2017), *PoEmotions Black History: Our Origins, Our Struggles, Our Future* (2018), *Flowers Grow & Butterflies Fly and Other Short Poems* (2019), and *PoEmotions: God and Faith* (2021). Patrick was born and raised in the Bronx, New York, where he still lives.

www.ingramcontent.com/pod-product-compliance
Lightning Source LLC
Chambersburg PA
CBHW072036110526
44592CB00012B/1443